To Pam

THE YORKSHIRE DALES TOP TEN

FIVE INDIVIDUAL WALKS
OR
80 MILES ON A CIRCULAR WALK OVER THE TEN HIGHEST PEAKS WITHIN THE YORKSHIRE DALES NATIONAL PARK.

AN
ESSENTIAL GUIDE TO
HELP YOU COMPLETE
THE
YORKSHIRE DALES TOP TEN

BRIAN SMAILES

Other books by the same author :-

JOHN O'GROATS TO LANDS END
ISBN 0-9526900-4-7

THE LAKELAND TOP TEN
ISBN 0-9526900-3-9

THE NATIONAL 3 PEAKS WALK
ISBN 0-9526900-7-1

THE NOVICES GUIDE TO THE YORKSHIRE 3 PEAKS WALK
ISBN 0-9526900-0-4

THE NOVICES GUIDE TO THE LYKE WAKE WALK
ISBN 0-9526900-1-2

THE COMPLETE ISLE OF WIGHT COASTAL FOOTPATH
ISBN 0-9526900-6-3

ISBN 0-9526900-5-5
First Published October 1999
CHALLENGE PUBLICATIONS
P.O. Box No. 132 Barnsley. S71 5YX

THE AUTHOR
BRIAN SMAILES

A record was established by him in June 1995 when he completed 5 continuous crossings of the Lyke Wake Walk across the North York Moors in 85 hours 50 minutes, a total of 210 miles over rough terrain.

Long distance running is one of his interests and he has completed 23 marathons and one 100km ultra run.

Other achievements include canoeing the Caledonian Canal 3 times and the river Wye, qualified scuba diving instructor and course director for Basic Expedition Leader Award courses.

Brian has travelled extensively around Great Britain and has experience of outdoor pursuits in all conditions.

CONTENTS

PLATES

The information recorded in this book is believed to be correct at publication. No Liabilities can be accepted for any inaccuracies which may be found. Anyone using this book should refer to their map and have some experience of map and compass use.

ACKNOWLEDGEMENTS

It is with thanks to the following people that this book has been published :-

The expedition team consisting of :-
Geoff Whittaker, Janet Crossley, Pam Smailes and Brian Smailes.

Geoff Whittaker and Janet Crossley for their help in the research of information.

Graham Fish for his help on the technical aspects of this book.

Julie Dalby for editing the text.

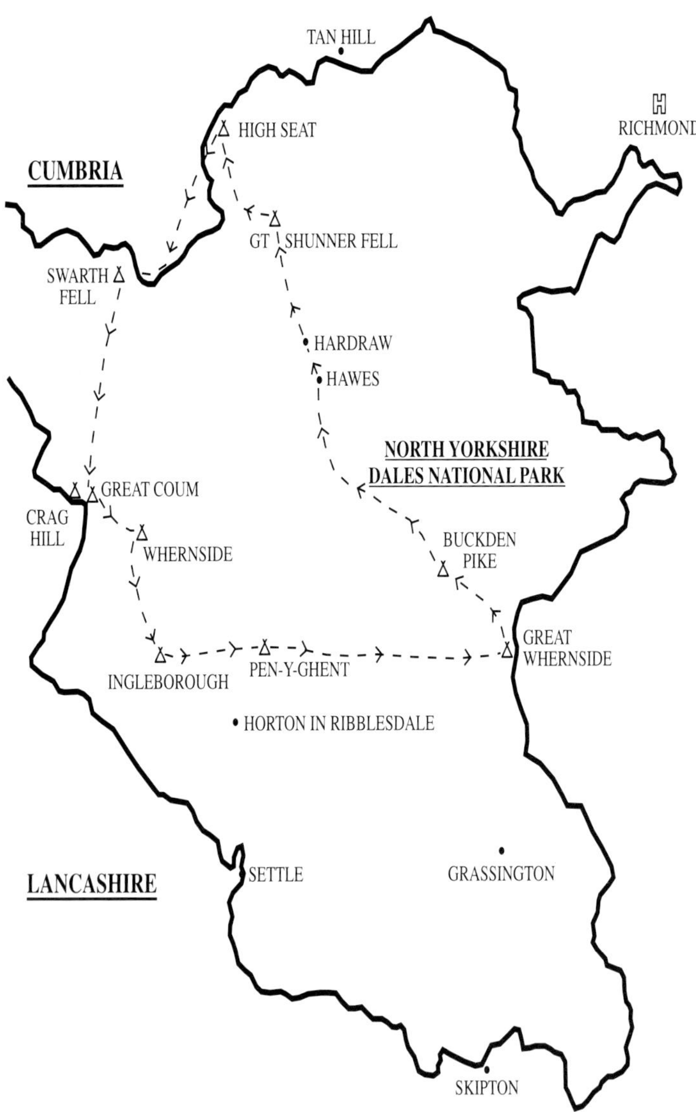
DURHAM
TAN HILL
RICHMOND
HIGH SEAT
CUMBRIA
GT SHUNNER FELL
SWARTH FELL
HARDRAW
HAWES
NORTH YORKSHIRE
DALES NATIONAL PARK
GREAT COUM
CRAG HILL
WHERNSIDE
BUCKDEN PIKE
GREAT WHERNSIDE
INGLEBOROUGH
PEN-Y-GHENT
HORTON IN RIBBLESDALE
LANCASHIRE
SETTLE
GRASSINGTON
SKIPTON

INTRODUCTION

The Yorkshire Dales Top Ten is a challenging but enjoyable walk over some of the best fells and peaks in Yorkshire. It consists of 80 miles of walking including 7231 metres of climbing. The terrain in some parts is inhospitable. This walk incorporates a climb to the summit of each of the ten highest peaks or fells some of which are on the Lancashire/Yorkshire border.

Take time to plan and study the route carefully. The walk itself is strenuous for people of any age. I cannot emphasise enough the planning and effort required to complete the ten highest peaks in Yorkshire safely. This book is laminated and compact enough to be carried on route along with the relevant maps.

I recommend starting this walk early each day to give you maximum daylight hours. It is possible to use campsites around the route. Details of these are given in the appendix.

There are five natural sections to this walk. Walkers may feel more able to complete this walk one section at a time rather than the full 80 mile circular walk. Whichever way you choose you will find it exhilarating and worthwhile to complete the ten highest peaks in Yorkshire.

A good understanding of the map and compass is required as most of the route is remote and unpopulated. To lose your way on these fells is dangerous, therefore respect for the outdoor environment must always be given and care taken.

All compass bearings referred to herein are given as magnetic and set in 1999. Magnetic North is estimated at 5° west of grid north in 1999 decreasing by approx ½° in four years. Check new maps for future reference.

Recommended Maps

Ordnance Survey	Yorkshire Dales No. 30 Northern and Central Areas
Ordnance Survey	Yorkshire Dales No. 2 Southern and Western Areas
Ordnance Survey	Howgill Fells No. 19 and Upper Eden Valley

All maps 1:25000 scale or 2½ inch to 1 mile

Although these are the recommended maps, you should ensure that whichever map you use it is relevant and up to date.

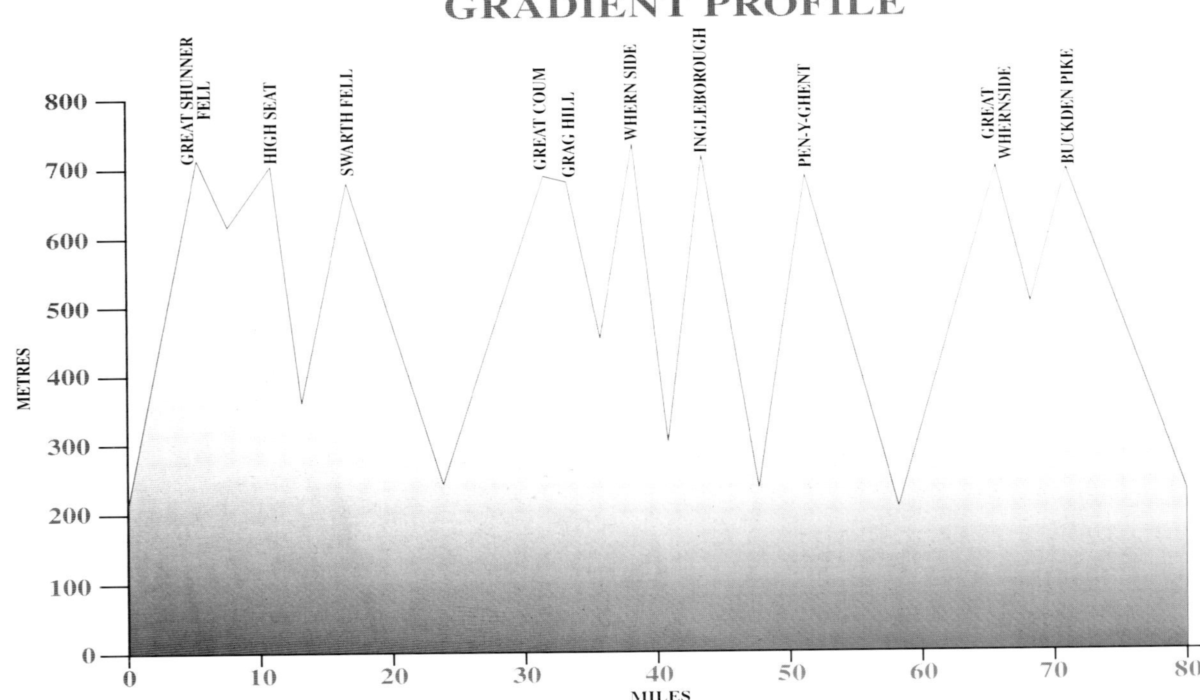
GRADIENT PROFILE
METRES
800
700
600
500
400
300
200
100
0
0
10
20
30
40
50
60
70
80
MILES
GREAT SHUNNER FELL
HIGH SEAT
SWARTH FELL
GREAT COUM
GRAG HILL
WHERN SIDE
INGLEBOROUGH
PEN-Y-GHENT
GREAT WHERNSIDE
BUCKDEN PIKE

WALK PREPARATION

It is essential for everyone undertaking this walk to be prepared in terms of physical preparation and also familiarisation of the route to be taken on the map.

Physical Preparation

The route described herein consists of over 7231 metres of climbing if you attempt the full circular walk. You should have a reasonable degree of fitness, even if you are only intending to ascend some of the peaks. Fitness training should incorporate leg muscle building and stamina training to help you when ascending mountains and in maintaining a reasonable steady pace whilst walking.

It is just as important to eat nutritious food before and during the event that will give you energy. Food such as rice, pasta, potatoes, apples and bananas are all good sources of energy. Take some high energy snacks and drinks with you to help give a constant supply of energy.

Familiarisation

The route to be taken whether it be the full circle or an individual peak should be studied in detail. Walking times and distances must be studied closely and a picture of the terrain to be encountered should be built up, in order to prepare you for the completion of the challenge ahead. A route card should be completed and a copy left with someone before you start walking (plate 1).

ROUTE CARD

FROM	TO	MAG/B	HEIGHT	DIST	TARGET	TIME

TOTAL TIME OUT = WALKING TIME + STOPPAGE TIME
ADD 30 MINS. FOR 300 MT. CLIMBED
WALKING SPEED 4KM/HR FOR MOUNTAINS

TIME OUT ______ TIME IN ______

LEADER ....

TEAM MEMBERS ....

....

Plate 1

EQUIPMENT

Walkers should already have a good knowledge of equipment needed for a walk such as this and most importantly how to use it. However I feel it is relevant to mention the technical merits and benefits of some of the more important clothing and equipment needed for this type of expedition. The items taken will obviously depend on whether a day walk or the full circular walk is being attempted.

Small Tent:-

This should be light enough to be carried as a backpacking tent and robust enough to withstand strong winds. A geodesic design will help in this instance. Make sure that the tent is waterproof and not just showerproof. Taped seams will help to both strengthen and keep the tent waterproof.

Sleeping Bag:-

This should be light and compact enough to fit into your rucksack - use a compression sack to help it to fit. Should you be purchasing a new sleeping bag make sure it is warm enough, possibly a 4 season bag.

Cooking Stove:-

When walking the full top ten route a stove will be needed. As you may experience strong winds depending on where you camp, a 'Trangia' type of stove is recommended. These are excellent in windy conditions and are quite light and compact to carry. They are fuelled by either methylated spirits or gas whichever you prefer. A minus point is the pan bases tend to become blackened when using methylated spirits.

Overjacket:-

This should ideally be wind/waterproof with elasticated cuffs and a zip up/velcro fastening front. There are many types on the market including fleece and other breathable fabrics. Allow space when fitting for jumpers and other clothing underneath. Deep pockets, a hood and a map pocket all help to give extra comfort and full use from the jacket.

Trousers:-

Ideally need to made be of fleece or cotton with plenty of zipped pockets and/or a map pocket. The important point is not to wear jeans as they draw the body's heat and chafe the skin when wet. They also take a long time to dry. Trousers can be cut off at the knees.

Gloves/Hat:-

These are essential on the peaks as you lose a lot of heat through your head and hands. Protect them and stay warm (plate 2).

THE BODY

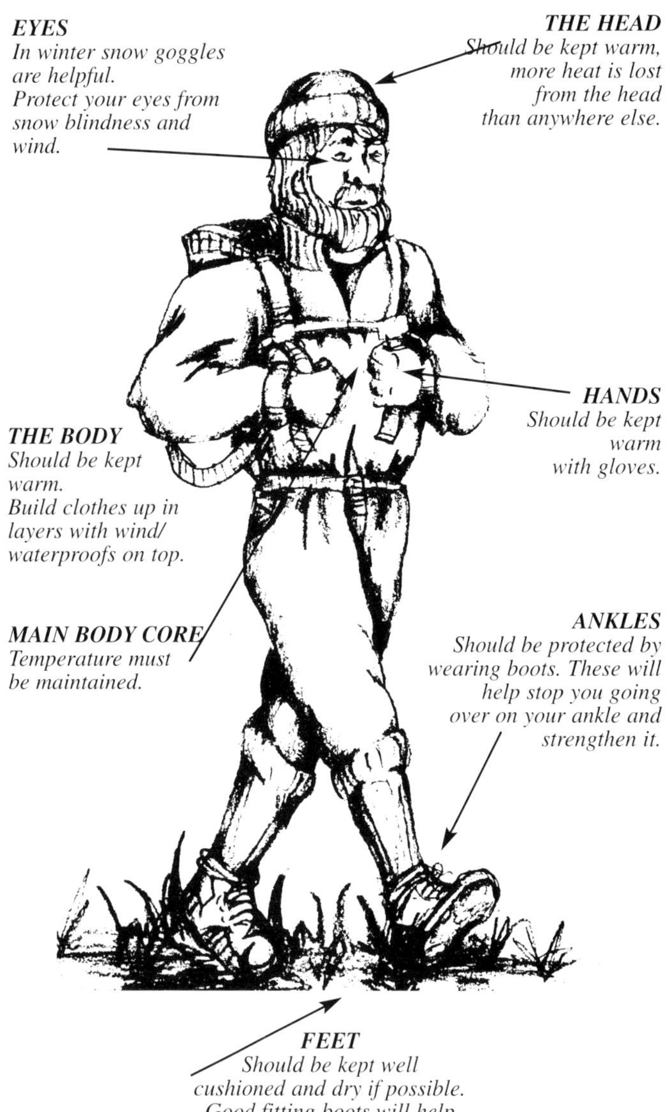

Plate 2

Rucksack:-

Should be large enough to hold all your personal and safety equipment with a pocket on either side and one in the top providing space for water bottles, maps, food etc. Take a full size rucksack if you are walking the full route or a day sack if you are only walking one or two mountains on a daily basis. Any rucksack should have wide padded shoulder straps and a waist belt to prevent movement. Place a large polythene liner inside the bag to keep your clothing dry.

Boots:-

These can be either leather, fabric or suede. Whichever you choose they should be comfortable, not too slack - not too tight. Ideally they should be waterproof, protect your ankles and have a sewn in tongue. Look after your boots and they will keep you dry and comfortable.

Essential Items:-

These items should be taken by all walkers whether it be a day walk or the full route:- Whistle, Compass, Maps, First Aid Kit, Torch including spare bulb and batteries, Survival Bag, Hat/Gloves, Food/Sweets/Nuts etc. Spare Clothing, Route Card, Water Bottle.

The following is a general suggested equipment list (which includes the above) and can be added to as necessary.

Plate 3

On the Pennine Way ascending to Great Shunner Fell

Plate 4

Checking your map and compass bearings on route to Swarth Fell near Black Paddock.

Tick

TENT/BIVI BAG
SLEEPING BAG
WATERPROOFS
RUCKSACK
WHISTLE
TORCH & SPARE BULB/BATTERIES
TIN OPENER
COMPASS
RELEVANT MAPS
HAT
GLOVES
BOOTS
EXTRA SWEATERS
PERSONAL CLOTHING
PENCIL/NOTEBOOK
ROUTE CARD
GAITERS
SPARE SOCKS
FIRST AID KIT
TOILETRIES
PLATE/CUP/CUTLERY
SLEEP MAT
WATER BOTTLE
SUNSCREEN
INSECT REPELLENT
FOOD
WATERPROOF MATCHES
STOVE/FUEL
PANS

MOUNTAIN SAFETY

To ensure the safety of all involved it is essential to plan your route carefully. Include sufficient equipment for your expedition that is able to stand up to the harsh conditions you could encounter on any of the peaks.

Bad weather may cause postponement or the need to find an alternative route or walk. It is better to abandon if there is a problem than to risk lives ascending a mountain in atrocious conditions or badly prepared. Complete a route card (plate 1), details of which should be left with someone who can monitor your progress and more importantly alert the rescue services if you are overdue.

More accidents happen on the return journey than on the outward one. This is due to a variety of reasons including complacency, exhaustion, lack of training/preparation and hypothermia. Many people do not realise that a calm sunny day in the valley can mean low cloud and gale force winds on the summit, add this to the wind chill factor and a badly prepared walker has problems. Bad weather can sweep in quickly. This walk, particularly the full route over the ten peaks is not for the inexperienced or the feint hearted.

Plate 5
The rough track along Nun House Outrake with Dentdale in the background on route to Great Coum

Plate 6
Walkers on the final ascent to the summit of Pen-Y-Ghent

Only walk routes that are within the capability of your party as one of the most common problems leading to accidents is walkers becoming separated from each other. There should be a party leader and that person should ensure the group walks at a sensible pace. Usually this is the speed of the slowest walker. Each person should carry a map and compass and know how to use them, along with a completed route card (plate 1) which has been drawn-up by the group as a whole beforehand.

Finally, be safe, stay together and be seen, take the correct equipment for the task and walk carefully.

THE MOUNTAIN CODE

Initially:-

Select equipment carefully.
Learn how to use it.
Be physically fit.
Know how to use a map and compass.
Where possible make an early start allowing time later in the day for bad weather.
Plan an alternative route for bad weather if possible.
Keep together.
Fill in route card and give a copy to a responsible person before you leave.
Check weather forecast.

HYPOTHERMIA

Hypothermia is caused when the body core temperature falls below 35°C. If a walker is not correctly prepared for the conditions or the equipment is not satisfactory then a combination of the cold, wet, exhaustion and the wind chill factor can give a walker hypothermia.

The signs and symptoms in descending order are:-

Shivering
Cold, pale and dry skin
Low body temperature
Irrational behaviour
A gradual slip into unconsciousness
Pulse and respiratory rate slow
Difficulty in detecting breathing & pulse when unconscious
Death

When on expedition there are ways of preventing hypothermia:-

1. Take extra sweaters to put on when cold.
2. Have suitable wind/waterproofs with you.
3. Build up body clothing in thin layers, adding on or taking off as necessary.
4. Take some food/hot drink or boiled sweets which produce energy and heat during digestion.
5. Wear balaclava/woolly hat to insulate the head, also gloves on hands (plate 2).
6. Shelter from the wind.

Take a survival bag and if conditions dictate, use it.

Plate 8

Ribblehead Viaduct to your left and your path from left to right leading towards Whernside on the Circular Walk No. 4

Plate 9

Ascending the Circular route No. 4 to Whernside. Your path is on the right with Force Gill Waterfall to the left.

In any type of emergency/accident situation it is always advisable to come off the mountain as soon as possible, such as in fog, snow or other bad conditions. The temperature difference between the valley and the summit can be several degrees. If the injured walker is able to move safely, going down the mountain is usually the best solution.

When conditions do not permit movement and if you are in a sheltered area, stay where you are until such time as conditions improve. It may be at this time you put on extra clothing and use survival bags.

Treatment for hypothermia:-

1. Provide extra clothing and shelter from the elements.
2. Bodily warmth of others helps in a gradual warming.
3. If well enough, come down into a warmer sheltered area.
4. Give hot drinks if conscious.
5. Give chocolate or sweets if the patient can still take food.
6. Do not rub the skin or use hot water bottle as this can cause a surge of blood from the central body core to the surface, this could prove fatal.
7. The casualty should be placed so that the head is slightly lower than the body.

Alcohol should not be consumed on any walk and should not be given to anyone who has hypothermia. The body temperature will be lowered as well as giving a false sense of security.

THE GEOLOGY OF THE DALES

The area around the Yorkshire Dales top ten is principally a limestone base dating from the carboniferous period although there is evidence below this of ordovician and silurian rock strata.

This limestone was formed when corals and sea creatures died, their shells thus creating this base. It took millions of years and numerous climatic changes to lay down this limestone layer. Further changes took place resulting in layers of sandstone, shale and mudstone being deposited through a glacial drift down the valleys.

To finish the geological strata of the area, a deposit of millstone grit was laid down in the tributaries of a river which flowed through the area on it's journey to the sea. Some peaks have this deposit of millstone grit covering them but the valleys gradually became covered with plants, trees and swamps resulting in some coal deposits being found and worked in former times in the North Yorkshire Dales area.

When rain, frost and sun weathers the limestone it becomes scarred with cracks and fissures, worn from the rock above and below ground, resulting in the many pot holes in the area.

Plate 10

The Car Park in Buckden Village, the path to Buckden Pike is in the centre. (Circular Walk No. 5).

Plate 11
The summit of Buckden Pike showing the 'Trig' Point

Around the Ingleborough plateau in particular you can see the fields of limestone outcrops with their fissures and gullies like spiders webs entrapping the careless feet of any walker who ventures over it in a casual manner. Walking in parts of the top ten will involve navigating between these limestone outcrops and over rock formations, so take care. I am sure you will find the geological structure of the area fascinating to see as I still do after many visits to the area.

GROUP 1
Great Shunner Fell, High Seat Circular Walk
Time to allow 11hrs
Total Distance 22½ miles
Start G.R. 867912
Map O.S. Outdoor Leisure 19

Leave Hardraw campsite and turn right past the tea room. After passing the outdoor centre turn right onto the Pennine Way. A sign opposite the turning points to Fossdale Moss, Cotterdale and Thwaite on the Pennine Way. Compass bearing 343°m at the turning. The farm lane is visible a long way in front (plate 3) as you ascend and is very stony in parts. You come to a stile, go over and continue. The first rise you come to is Little Fell at 455 metres (Ht).

Next along the route is Hearne Top. The route is marked by a pile of stones. Bear right, still on the Pennine Way. The track becomes narrower and sometimes disappears but is marked by further piles of stones.

Before the summit of Great Shunner Fell there is a flat area and the path has slabs of stone over the wet sections. Climb a stile over the wire fence leading to the summit where there is a 'trig' point, number 7747, built into a 4 way wind shelter.

To walk to High Seat you return to the stile over the wire fence, then take a bearing of 293°m. There is no definitive path but your route takes you over thick grass onto lower ground where you will meet and follow a wire boundary fence in the general direction of Hugh Seat before ascending to High Seat which may be seen in the distance.

Before reaching the summit of Hugh Seat, cross a stile, ascend to another stile then up a short steep ascent to the summit.

Leaving Hugh Seat summit, on bearing 334°m, walk towards a pile of stones 1500 metres ahead, G.R. 802003. At this pile of stones take bearing 111°m to High Seat. There is no visible path for most of this route so compass, map and visual orientation is recommended. High Seat is marked with a pile of stones on each side of the highest ground.

Re-trace your steps to the first pile of stones and on bearing 200°m walk to a cairn in the distance. Pass to the right of Hugh Seat and below it, walking over course grass and heather. Once in the valley below Hugh Seat there is a cairn marked at Burnt Crag. Keep to the west of it and walk towards Black Paddock and High Rigg Well (plate 4). Look for the stream and follow this down the valley to Hell Gill Bridge. Cross over a small stone bridge and turn left at Hell Gill Bridge, bearing 155°m, onto a distinctive path known as 'The Highway'. There are shake holes on both sides of the path, it is a pleasant walk from here back to Hardraw.

Follow the path alongside a wall until you reach a forest on your left, west of Cotterdale. At the corner of the forest walk down a short steep bank then through a swing gate to meet the A684 road at the bottom of the hill. Turn left and walk with care along the road to the campsite at Hardraw.

GROUP 2
Swarth Fell Circular Walk
Time to allow 3hrs 15mins
Total Distance 8.9miles
Start G.R. 778963
Map O.S. Outdoor Leisure 19

Start from Aisgill Moor cottages where there is a good tea room with crafts. Walk approximately 650 metres along the road to just before Cotegill Bridge where there is a 5 bar gate leading into a field on your left. Swarth Fell summit is up above the field.

There is no definitive path to the summit only coarse grass covering the foothills. Pick the best route up to the shoulder and refer to your map, approximate bearing 265°m. This should take you to the shoulder just under the summit. Bear right up to a col at the northern end of Swarth Fell, look for a path and a stone wall which you can follow. This leads to the summit on bearing 152°m from the stone wall. The grass covered summit is scattered with loose stones. A pile of stones and a wind shelter marks the summit.

Leaving Swarth Fell summit to return to Aisgill Moor cottages, follow the line of the fence at the far end of the flat plateau summit on bearing 136°m descending towards The Tongue. Pick up a path just before Turner Hill that leads from East House at G.R. 782941, which is approximately 3850 metres from the summit. The ground is reasonably flat and in a small col.

Turn left onto this path in a northerly direction. This path appears more like a narrow sheep track for most of the way. Following this path will take you back to Aisgill Moor cottages. The path is undulating in a downhill direction. You should see the cottages, road and railway line running nearly parallel with your path ahead of you.

GROUP 3
Great Coum and Crag Hill Circular Walk
Time to allow 3hrs
Total Distance 5.91miles
Start G.R. 720854
Map O.S. Outdoor Leisure 2

Start from Peacock Hill where a sign points to Nun House Outrake, on a general bearing of 232°m. This is a metalled road which soon becomes a very stony and rutted wide track (plate 5), ascending towards Great Coum. On reaching a fork in the path do not take Green Lane track to your right, instead follow the left path, then 50 metres after turning the bend bear off at 221°m. Ascend over the grass for 750 metres towards Great Coum summit. You will bear round to the right of Great Coum near the disused coal pits to avoid the steep slopes in front, then up towards the summit.

Great Coum's summit is grassy with stone walls, a wire fence and a small pile of stones marking it. A grass path runs alongside the stone wall to Crag Hill summit for 1000 metres. There is a 'trig' point on Crag Hill number 5661.

When leaving Crag Hill retrace your steps to Great Coum summit, from there take a bearing 114°m descending near a stone wall down the grass hillside to the old track Nun House Outrake. On reaching this obvious rutted track, turn left following this track for 1500 metres, rejoining the original path you ascended on. When you reach the fork in the path turn right back to Peacock Hill on Nun House Outrake.

GROUP 4
Pen-y-ghent, Whernside, Ingleborough Circular Walk
Time to allow 11½hrs
Total Distance 25miles
Start G.R. 808726
Map O.S. Outdoor Leisure 2

Turn right from the car park in Horton in Ribblesdale and proceed to the Pen-y-ghent café/Tourist Information Centre which is about 45 metres along the road on your right. After using the free safety service and purchasing items in the shop, turn right and continue along towards the church which you will see at the south end of the village. You will pass Holme Farm campsite on your right, cross the road.

Just past the campsite, turn left through a gate into a small field. The church is a short distance away. Proceed through the next gate in front of you then turn left. You will see a wooden bridge over the stream about 35 metres further on. Cross over it then turn left onto a metalled road along by the local school.

Continue on the metalled road until you come to a farm where there is a signpost pointing to Pen-y-ghent summit 1700 metres. Turn left here, over a stile and up by a stone wall. The grass path now starts to go steeply uphill, there are many ruts in the path.

Arriving at some stone steps in the wall ahead of you, Pen-y-ghent appears directly in front now. Over another wall there is a large stone outcrop with some steps carved in it, go up these and continue generally along the side of the stone wall.

Looking back you can see Ingleborough in the distance with Horton in the valley and the quarry behind. At the base of Pen-y-ghent there are some steps as you continue to ascend steeply. Over two more stiles and you now have a view of the south side of Pen-y-ghent.

The shale and stone path to the summit is steep and care should be taken (plate 6). As you approach there are some steep steps up the large rock outcrop after where the path starts to flatten out before coming to a walkway. The 'trig' point is in front of you on the summit. Enjoy the view in all directions.

Near the triangulation pillar is a stile over the stone wall, go over this and you will see your path going downhill, bearing 335°m, follow the path for 300 metres until it begins to turn right on an approximate bearing of 27°m. N.B. this path is reasonably obvious.

Halfway down the hill you will see another distinct, white looking path on your left, which leads back to Horton in Ribblesdale and is known as the Pennine Way. This is useful if you decide to climb only one hill then return. After passing this path on your left continue on the main route which veers left for a short distance on bearing 307°m (from the path junction) then runs nearly parallel with the previous path that leads back to Horton. The paths are about 90 metres apart. Your route is grassy and you can usually see the worn path in the distance leading to Ribblehead with Whernside directly behind it.

After following this path you arrive at a wet and boggy section, after crossing this and a small stream beyond you will see a stone wall in front. Go over the stile and continue downhill to a second stream, then over two more stiles, eventually coming to a wider stream. This is a pleasant area for picnics on route.

After crossing the wide stream and going over the numerous undulating small hills you arrive at the main area of natural springs known as Black Dub Moss. This is usually very wet even in summer, so careful navigation around and over this 550 metres stretch of numerous ditches, gullies and peat bog, is essential.

Proceed up the small hill, continuing in the general direction of Ribblehead. It is undulating for another mile with good views all around. Walk along the side of the stone wall in front of you and across a grass field, keeping the limestone rock on your left. There are some fir trees on your left then another opening in the stone wall. The path turns to gravel and grass before joining another narrow road leading to a farm on your right. At the junction of the path and narrow road follow a sign saying footpath only, no cycling. Cross over the road and down the path still heading towards Ribblehead Viaduct.

Go over a stile and follow a rutted farmers track. You see a stone wall on your left and as the path bends around to the right, branch off across the grass along by the side of the wall. You go through a gate following the undulating path, in parts the path is good then others just a farmers track.

Plate 7

The refreshment stop near Ribblehead viaduct with Ingleborough on the left side. (Circular Walk No. 4)

Turn left over a stile, then across a field, before turning right through the farmyard. Go over the next stile beside the farmhouse onto a good road. Follow the signpost pointing to Ribblehead.

Pass over a bridge which spans a wide river and soon you start to ascend on a farm track past another farm. As you pass the farm there is a tarmac road. On your left is a spring with some good refreshing drinking water. Follow the tarmac road up to the main road, turn right and walk down to Ribblehead Viaduct (plate 7). At the junction there is a sign saying Ingleton to your left. You go straight across towards the viaduct, which has 24 arches.

This junction has a stream and often a refreshments van and is another good picnic area. Carry on towards the viaduct keeping to the right of it (plate 8) follow the path to the far end before turning right up some stone steps with a stone wall on your left. The Settle/Carlisle Railway is parallel with your path.

Here, the path turns to shale chippings as you proceed around the northerly side of Whernside. You come to a stile, go over and continue on this undulating path for 800 metres. As you proceed you will pass Blea Moor Signal Box and the ruins of the old railway house. When walking this section you go over two small brooks, the path is very stony and uneven. You then cross a wide stream that is covered with stones but easily passable.

Nearing a stone wall the path turns to grass. Continue on this and as you start to ascend you will see the path which you need to take ahead of you.

Follow the path between the stone walls, with Blea Moor Tunnel on your right and the aqueduct on the left, then go over a stile and continue towards the summit. A signpost just after the gate shows V.W.Dentdale 4 miles in your direction of travel.

On the left you will see Force Gill Waterfall (plate 9). You are climbing anti-clockwise up Whernside and about halfway up there is another stile over a wire fence. The path bears off left towards the summit. Continue further on a stony path, then on stone slabs nearly to the summit where Pen-y-ghent can be seen clearly to your left and Ingleborough straight ahead. Below Whernside there is a small tarn called Greensett Tarn, which looks quite inviting on a hot day. On the summit on a clear day you can see Morecambe Bay to your right with the mountains of the Lake District to your extreme right. The 'trig' point on Whernside summit is number 2982.

Continue from the summit in the same direction, bearing 201°m towards Ingleborough. The limestone plateau that surrounds Ingleborough can clearly be seen. Follow the very stony and uneven path carefully down the side of the stone wall for 1220 metres, turn left here on bearing 162°m taking the obvious path towards Bruntscar.

When taking the path off Whernside extreme care should be taken as the stone path is steep and dangerous for about 60 metres, one slip can send you rolling down the hill. Further down the path becomes gravel and easier to walk on.

Go over two stiles and turn left just past the farm building. Follow the metalled road with a small wooded area in front. This leads to another farm building and eventually the main road. Turn left here and you will see the Old Hill Inn and the campsite in the area known as Chapel le Dale. This is a good refreshment stop.

Just past the Old Hill Inn there is a small stile on your right. Go over this and cross the field, then over a number of stiles and several fields in the general direction of Ingleborough. On your left side as you proceed on a stone chipping path, you pass numerous limestone outcrops.

Passing a large pit or disused quarry on your left, you approach the base of Ingleborough, called Humphrey Bottom. Continue up to a stone wall where the path turns right. Cross over a stile on your left and you are on a wooden boarded path which is there to combat erosion. Continue on this to the base of Ingleborough.

At the end of the wooden boarded path take the steep climb up to the summit along a small stream. This zig-zag path is very steep and uneven, so take care. Nearing the summit a signpost states National Nature Reserve and Welcome to Ingleborough.

Go through a swing gate and you have your last short steep climb to the summit. At the top of the steps on your left is the path you need to take you back to Horton in Ribblesdale, marked by a cairn. Continue up the steep rocky outcrop to two cairns, with a 4-way wind shelter in view directly ahead on the summit.

The summit is flat but very rocky. There is a triangulation pillar and the 4-way shelter which gives some respite from the wind. On the top of it is a plaque depicting the views in all directions. In misty conditions or if disorientated, a compass bearing from the wind break of 80°m should take you back to the two cairns. Retrace your steps to the cairn marking the path to Horton which leads off right then take a compass bearing of 100°m to go downhill. The path has been repaired in parts over recent years and can be muddy in places.

Take the grass path with Pen-y-ghent in front and Horton down in the valley. Go over a stile. A sign pointing to Horton is just past it, followed by a large outcrop of limestone. This path runs between the limestone and undulating small hills, continue in a straight line towards Horton and Pen-y-ghent. Another signpost points back to Ingleborough and Horton 1½ miles (experience says it could be further), also to Sellside and Clapham.

Go over another stile and onto a stony path, through an opening in the stone wall, leading to a large expanse of limestone rocks. The path turns to the right, pick out your path here carefully. The large expanse of limestone rock diminishes making way for fields, usually containing animals.

Cross the fields following the narrow, undulating, worn trail with numerous stiles over the stone walls. As you approach the railway line you see a sign for Horton in Ribblesdale at the small station. Cross the line with care and continue down the path and along the road ahead towards the car park in the village.

Cross the small bridge over the river on your right - you are back in the car park. Return to the café and 'clock back in'.

GROUP 5
Buckden Pike, Great Whernside Circular Walk
Time to allow 6hrs
Total Distance 17.84miles
Start G.R. 942774
Map O.S. Outdoor Leisure 30

Start from the main car park in Buckden (a pay and display car park). The path to Buckden Pike leads out of the car park through a gate near a post box (plate 10). A sign here points to Buckden Pike and Cray High Bridge. The path is shale and stone ascending to some trees. Continue along the side of a stone wall where the path becomes very stony. You come to a farm gate, go through and continue close to the wall on your left.

You come to a sign pointing to Buckden Pike, which is beside the second stone wall on your right, when ascending. Do not turn on the track that bears off to the right just before the sign but go through the metal gate at the signpost and ascend diagonally across a field. The path is grass and you may see the worn path ahead. Pass through another metal gate, a sign here states National Trust Upper Wharfedale. The path leads to another opening in a stone wall and continues to ascend. The path from the car park to the summit is quite well defined.

Walk through another opening in a stone wall. The path becomes more uneven here with a mixture of grass and stone. Pass over another crumbling stone wall as you approach the upper side of Buckden Pike. Ahead you see another wall with a wooden gate, go through. Walk over the wet boggy section ahead and then on the stony path which is near the ridge.

Plate 12
The Memorial Cross on the decent from Buckden Pike towards Great Whernside.

Walk along the expanse of grass and beside the wall to reach the summit where a pile of stones and a white 'trig' point, number 5520 (plate 11) can be found. On a clear day views of Pen-y-ghent, Whernside and Ingleborough are visible. A wooden sign points back to Buckden.

Climb over the stile near the 'trig' point and take bearing 175°m from the stile to confirm your route. Follow the worn path which leads alongside the stone wall from Buckden Pike. On a clear day Great Whernside can be seen. Follow the wall along and you come to a monument, in memory of an airman and a plane crash (plate 12). As you begin to descend into the valley your path leads around the stone wall in the general direction of Great Whernside. There may be some wet areas as you descend.

Climb over a stile. The grass path continues along side the wall. You will reach another stile but do not go over, instead bear left here and you will soon see the path in front leading to a road in the valley with a cattle grid. Descending to the road the wall stops part way down and the path tends to be grass and undulating.

Cross the road and follow the signpost to Great Whernside. Follow the narrow path up the hillside, the first part of which is small mounds of grass. You will then come to an opening in the wall with 2 steps up and a small gate. Pass through and continue on a short steep ascent on a stony path. Climb over another stile and you should see countless large stones on a plateau known as Blackfell Top where a wind shelter can be found.

Plate 13

Kettlewell Village in the centre with the path descending from Great Whernside on the left.

Continue approximately 1000 metres along the flat plateau to Great Whernside summit and the 'trig' point number 2976. The summit consists of large stones on one side and grass on the other.

Your route now descends just below the 'trig' point to Hag Dyke then Kettlewell, bearing 254°m. There are some piles of stones halfway down. Hag Dyke is just below and is a building belonging to a scout group.

On reaching Hag Dyke go through the cottage grounds then through a farm gate where the path descends by a wall to Kettlewell. A sign states footpath Kettlewell and bridleway Kettlewell. Take the footpath, which is a more direct route.

Continue to descend and you should see Kettlewell in the valley (plate 13). Pass through 2 gates and over a stile. There is a campsite just as you enter the village. Follow the path then the road through Kettlewell to the main bridge near the car park. Cross over the main bridge in Kettlewell then turn right and follow the Dales Way back to Buckden car park. The path is very obvious as it runs parallel with the river back to Buckden. You go through numerous gates and over stiles on this flat path which is very popular with walkers.

When you reach the turning to Buckden there is a sign pointing to Buckden. Follow the path to a bridge then turn right to return to the car park.

This section is the complete circular walk to be attempted over at least 3 days.

THE YORKSHIRE DALES TOP TEN FULL CIRCULAR WALK

Leave Hardraw campsite and turn right past the tea room. After passing the outdoor centre turn right onto the Pennine Way. A sign opposite the turning points to Fossdale Moss, Cotterdale and Thwaite on the Pennine Way. Compass bearing 343°m at the turning. The farm lane is visible a long way in front (plate 3) as you ascend and is very stony in parts. You come to a stile, go over and continue. The first rise you come to is Little Fell 455 metres (Ht.)

Next along the route is Hearne Top. The route is marked by a pile of stones. Bear right, still on the Pennine Way. The track becomes narrower and sometimes disappears but is marked by futher piles of stones.

Before the summit of Great Shunner Fell there is a flat area and the path has slabs of stone over the wet sections. Climb a stile over the wire fence leading to the summit where there is a 'trig' point, number 7747, built into a 4 way wind shelter.

To walk to High Seat you return to the stile over the wire fence, then take a bearing of 293°m. There is no definitive path but your route takes you over thick grass onto lower ground where you will meet a wire boundary fence which you walk alongside in the general direction of Hugh Seat before ascending to High Seat which you may be able to see in the distance.

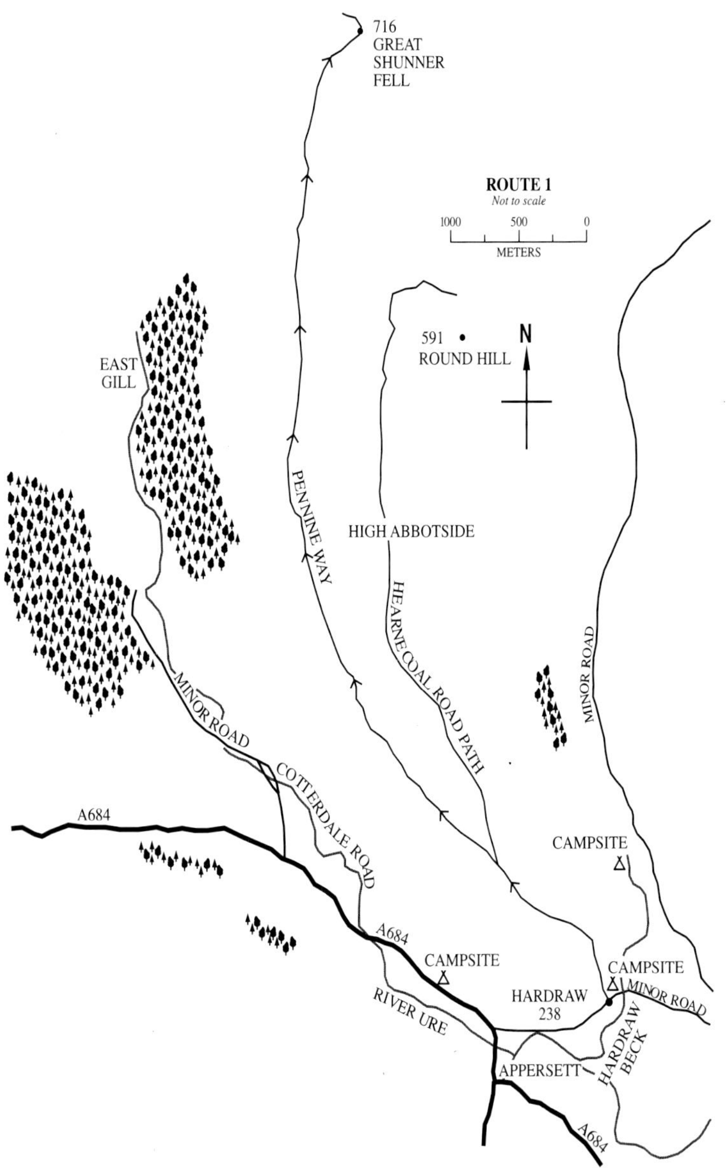
716
GREAT
SHUNNER
FELL
ROUTE 1
Not to scale
1000
500
0
METERS
591
ROUND HILL
N
EAST
GILL
PENNINE WAY
HIGH ABBOTSIDE
HEARNE COAL ROAD PATH
MINOR ROAD
MINOR ROAD
COTTERDALE ROAD
A684
CAMPSITE
A684
CAMPSITE
CAMPSITE
HARDRAW
238
MINOR ROAD
RIVER URE
HARDRAW
BECK
APPERSETT
A684

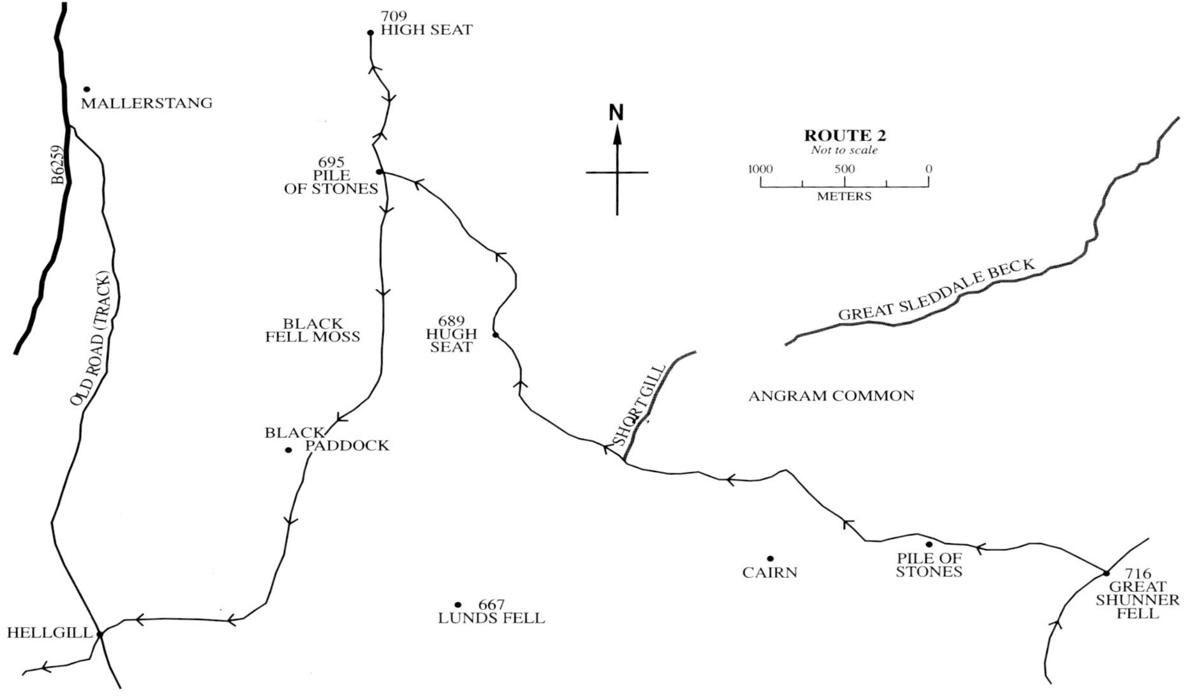

ROUTE 2
Not to scale
1000
500
0
METERS
N
709 HIGH SEAT
MALLERSTANG
B6259
695 PILE OF STONES
OLD ROAD (TRACK)
BLACK FELL MOSS
689 HUGH SEAT
GREAT SLEDDALE BECK
SHORTGILL
ANGRAM COMMON
BLACK PADDOCK
CAIRN
PILE OF STONES
716 GREAT SHUNNER FELL
667 LUNDS FELL
HELLGILL

Before reaching the summit of Hugh Seat, cross a stile, ascend to another stile then up a short steep ascent to the summit.

Leaving Hugh Seat summit, on bearing 334°m, walk towards a pile of stones 1500 metres ahead, G.R. 802003. At this pile of stones take bearing 111°m to High Seat. There is no visible path for most of this route so compass, map and visual orientation is recommended. High Seat is marked with a pile of stones on each side of the highest ground.

Re-trace your steps to the first pile of stones and on bearing 200°m walk to a cairn in the distance. Pass to the right of Hugh Seat and below it, walking over course grass and heather. Once in the valley below Hugh Seat there is a cairn marked at Burnt Crag. Keep to the west of it and walk towards Black Paddock and High Rigg Well (plate 4). Look for the stream and follow this down the valley to Hell Gill Bridge. Cross over this small stone bridge and walk down the farm track to Aisgill Moor Cottages, possibly stopping off at the tea room for refreshments.

Turn right and walk approximately 650 metres along the road to just before Cotegill Bridge where there is a 5 bar gate leading into a field on your left. Swarth Fell summit is up above the field.

There is no definitive path to the summit only coarse grass covering the foothills. Pick the best route up to the shoulder and refer to your map, approximate bearing 265°m. This should take you to the shoulder just under the summit. Bear right up

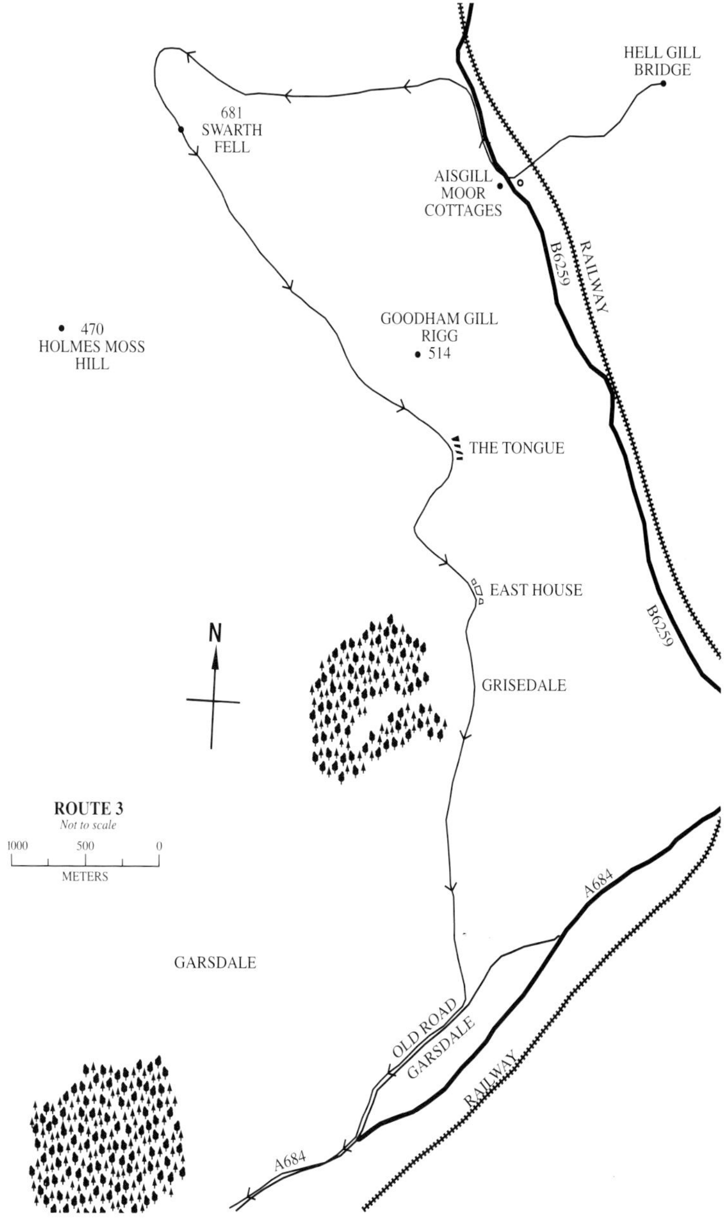
HELL GILL
BRIDGE
681
SWARTH
FELL
AISGILL
MOOR
COTTAGES
B6259
RAILWAY
GOODHAM GILL
RIGG
514
470
HOLMES MOSS
HILL
THE TONGUE
EAST HOUSE
B6259
N
GRISEDALE
ROUTE 3
Not to scale
1000
500
0
METERS
A684
GARSDALE
OLD ROAD
GARSDALE
RAILWAY
A684

to a col at the northern end of Swarth Fell, look for a path and a stone wall which you can follow. This leads to the summit on bearing 152°m from the stone wall. The grass covered summit is scattered with loose stones. A pile of stones and a wind shelter marks the summit.

On leaving Swarth Fell summit, follow the line of the fence at the far end of the flat plateau summit towards East House, bearing 149°m. When descending by the fence there is a stile on your right halfway down, go over and descend to the bottom corner of the field where there is a farm gate. Walk through, still descending towards East House.

You meet a farm track, turn left and continue on this track to East House. When you reach East House G.R. 777938 a single track road begins. Walk on this road past the farms and over cattle grids south for 2080 metres to meet Old Road. Turn right here walking for 1000 metres to reach the A684. Turn right again on the A684 walking for a further 1700 metres to Dandra Garth.

Look for a sign saying Cowgill 2 miles. There is a farm gate at the side of the A684 which has Dandra Garth on the gate G.R. 753897. Walk through the farm buildings, bearing left, then start to ascend. Whilst ascending, you come to a forest where the stony path winds it's way up and through a narrow part before arriving at the corner of a larger forest. A sign states 'Fire Danger', continue on the left path, do not bend round to the right. Your path ascends along the side of the forest before bearing off to your left. Walk through a gate into a boggy section where the path tends to disappear in parts.

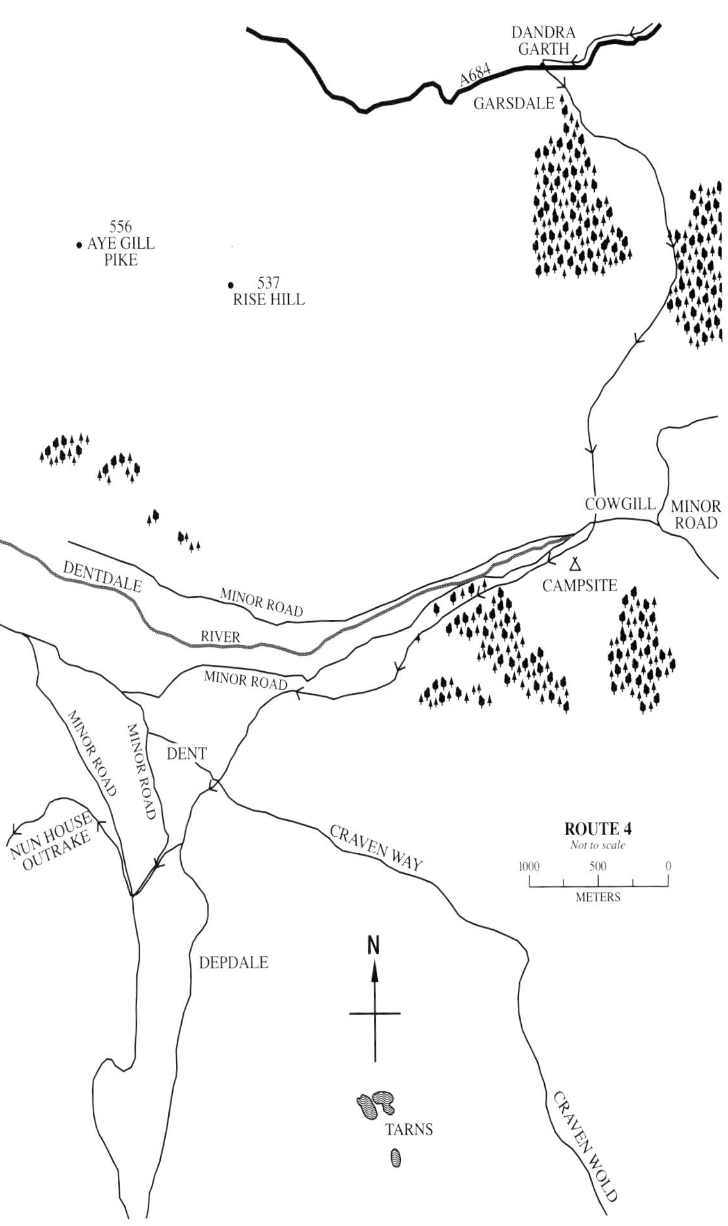
DANDRA GARTH
A684
GARSDALE
556
AYE GILL PIKE
537
RISE HILL
COWGILL
MINOR ROAD
CAMPSITE
DENTDALE
MINOR ROAD
RIVER
MINOR ROAD
DENT
MINOR ROAD
MINOR ROAD
NUN HOUSE OUTRAKE
CRAVEN WAY
ROUTE 4
Not to scale
1000
500
0
METERS
N
DEPDALE
TARNS
CRAVEN WOLD

There is a stone wall on your left now as you ascend the hillside. The path bears to the left and you come to a stream, cross it and you should see some vehicle tracks in the path in places. As you ascend the path meets the side of a stone wall on your left. Continue to walk straight ahead, as the wall bears off to the left. The ground levels out and you see a forest slightly to your left and Whernside in the distance ahead. Walk through a possible boggy section to the right side of the forest.

You see a farm track and a metal gate between 2 stone walls, walk through and descend on a grass, then stone and shale path to Cowgill. This section is particularly enjoyable. You arrive at 2 gates, take the left one around the side of a small wood, then follow it into Cowgill. You emerge onto the road at Cowgill at the side of the churchyard. A campsite is opposite on the other side of the stream.

Turn right at the road, over a small bridge and past Yewgales Bridge Campsite, picking up the Dales Way. Walk on the road for 450 metres, then bear left, through a gate in front of you with a signpost and yellow arrow pointing to Laithes Bank 1½ miles. The path takes you along the lower side of the forest in front. Follow the distinctive path over at least 6 stiles still staying on the Dales Way, which runs parallel with the road on your right, until you reach Laithbank.

Near Laithbank you go through a wooden gate beside a small stream before crossing a field and passing a barn. There is a small stile and a sign pointing to Dales Way. Do not take the Dales Way path to your right but take the left path, bearing

241°m, then immediate left again bearing 216°m. There is another sign stating footpath to your left, beside some farm buildings. Go through a narrow opening between a wall then ascend steeply up over a hill. Drop down again aiming for Rig End and Outrake Foot.

Your path passes a farm building and across a field to another sign saying footpath and Sike Fold ahead. Turn off left over the stile and cross a short field and small stream. Another sign states Rig End, follow this to your left. Ascend diagonally to a stile over the stone wall, then over another stile. Keep ascending over the hill then off to your right following the farm track down at Deepdale Lane. Turn right on Deepdale Lane and pick up another path on your left to Butter Pots, which leads onto Nun House Outrake.

Your new path leads along Nun House Outrake on bearing 232°m. This is a short metalled road which soon becomes a very stony and rutted wide track (plate 5) ascending towards Great Coum. On reaching a fork in the path do not take Green Lane track to your right, instead follow the left path, then 50 metres after turning the bend bear off at 221°m. Ascend over the grass for 750 metres towards Great Coum summit. You will bear round to the right of Great Coum near the disused coal pits to avoid the steep slopes in front, then up towards the summit.

Great Coum's summit is grassy with stone walls a wire fence and a small pile of stones marking it. A grass path runs alongside the stone wall to Crag Hill summit for 1000 metres. There is a 'trig' point on Crag Hill, number 5661.

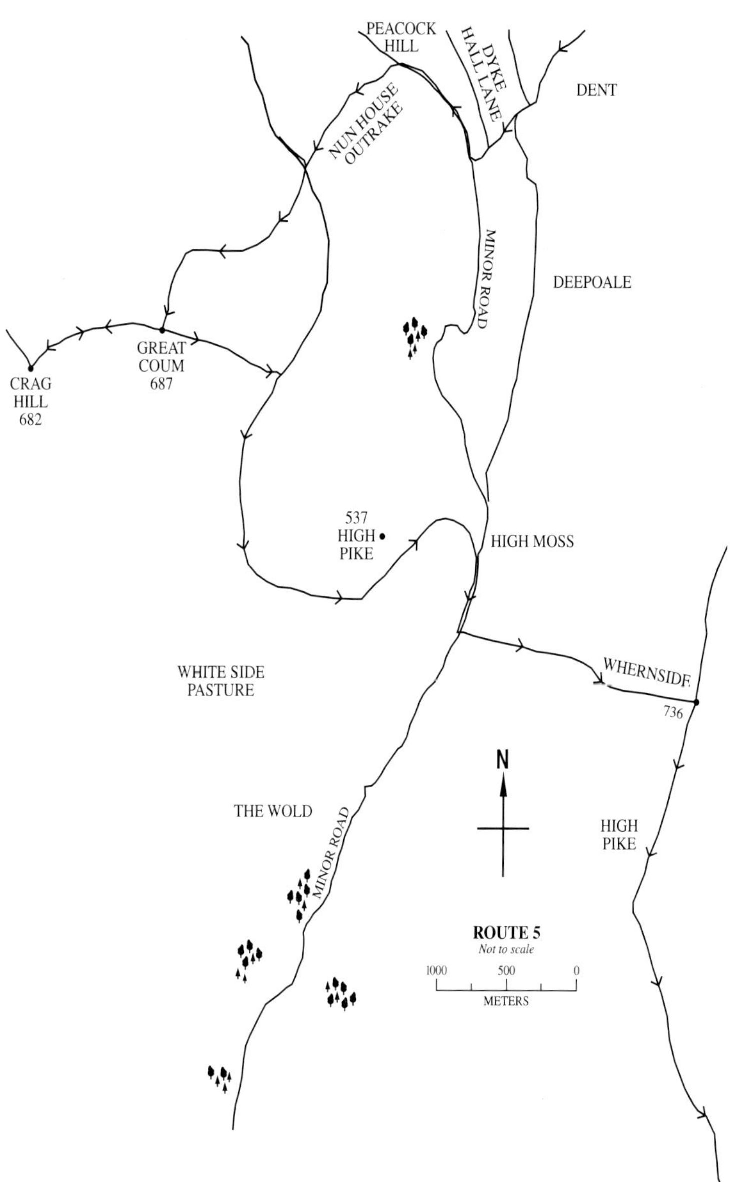
PEACOCK HILL
DYKE HALL LANE
DENT
NUN HOUSE OUTRAKE
MINOR ROAD
DEEPOALE
GREAT COUM 687
CRAG HILL 682
537 HIGH PIKE
HIGH MOSS
WHITE SIDE PASTURE
WHERNSIDE
736
N
THE WOLD
MINOR ROAD
HIGH PIKE
ROUTE 5
Not to scale
1000 500 0
METERS

When leaving Crag Hill retrace your steps to Great Coum summit, from there take a bearing 114°m descending near a stone wall down the grass hillside to the old track Nun House Outrake. On reaching this obvious rutted track turn right following it for 3000 metres until you reach the minor road. Turn right on this road and walk 500 metres before turning left on an obvious path, bearing 103°m along the side of a stone wall to Whernside. This path ascends steeply but is virtually straight for 1170 metres before turning right briefly then back on the previous direction of 103°m to arrive at the 'trig' point on Whernside summit.

On the summit on a clear day you can see Morecambe Bay to your right and the mountains of the Lake District to your extreme right. The 'trig' point on Whernside summit is number 2982.

Continue from the summit bearing 201°m towards Ingleborough. The limestone plateau that surrounds Ingleborough can clearly be seen. Follow the very stony and uneven path carefully along the side of the stone wall for 1220 metres, turn left here on bearing 162°m taking the obvious path towards Bruntscar.

When taking the path off Whernside extreme care should be taken as the stone path is steep and dangerous for about 60 metres, one slip can send you rolling down the hill. Further down the path becomes gravel and easier to walk on.

Go over two stiles and turn left just past the farm building. Follow the metalled road with a small wooded area in front. This leads to another farm building and eventually the main road. Turn left here and you will see the Old Hill Inn and the campsite in an area known as Chapel le Dale. This is a good refreshment stop.

Just past the Old Hill Inn there is a stile on your right. Go over this and cross the field, then over a number of stiles and several fields in the general direction of Ingleborough. On your left side as you proceed on a stone chipping path, you pass numerous limestone outcrops.

Passing a large pit or disused quarry on your left, you approach the base of Ingleborough, called Humphrey Bottom. Continue up to a stone wall where the path turns right. Cross over a stile on your left and you are on a wooden boarded path which is there to combat erosion. Continue on this to the base of Ingleborough.

At the end of the wooden boarded path you will see a steep climb up to the summit along a small stream. This zig-zag path is very steep and uneven, so take care. Nearing the summit a signpost states National Nature Reserve and Welcome to Ingleborough.

Go through a swing gate and you have your last short steep climb to the summit. At the top of the steps on your left is the path you need to take you back to Horton in Ribblesdale, marked by a cairn. Continue up the steep rocky outcrop to two cairns, with a 4-way wind shelter in view directly ahead on the summit.

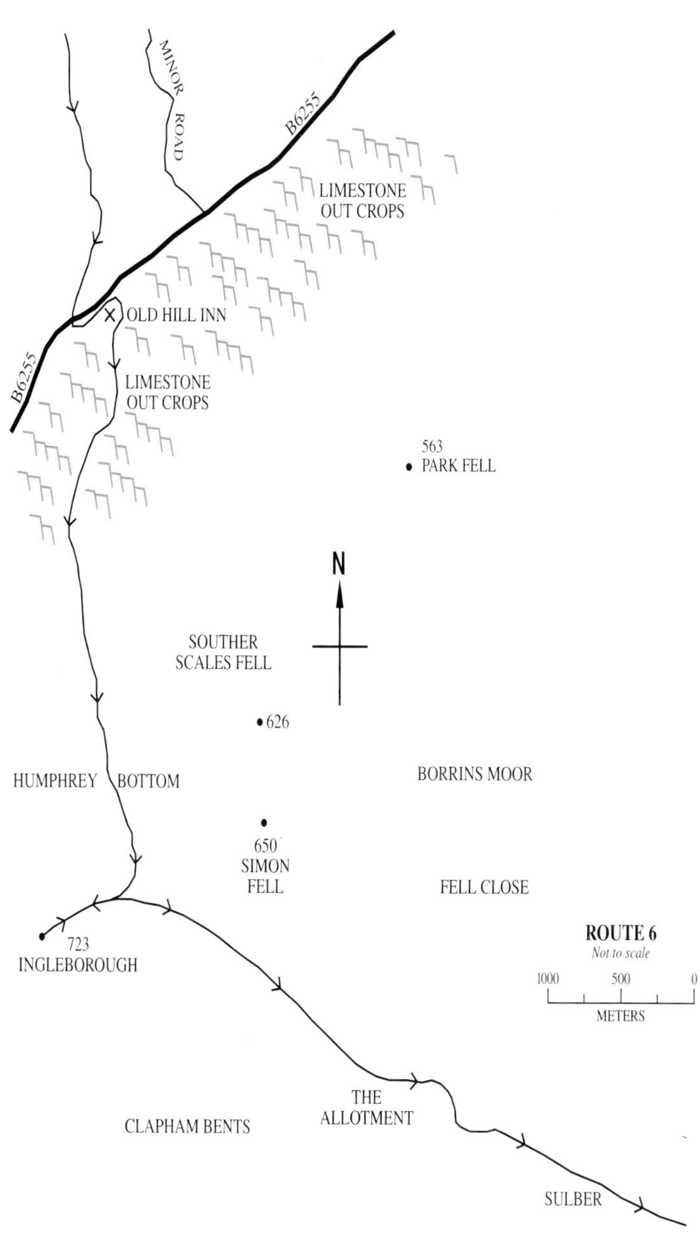
MINOR ROAD
B6255
LIMESTONE OUT CROPS
OLD HILL INN
B6255
LIMESTONE OUT CROPS
563
PARK FELL
N
SOUTHER SCALES FELL
626
HUMPHREY BOTTOM
BORRINS MOOR
650
SIMON FELL
FELL CLOSE
723
INGLEBOROUGH
ROUTE 6
Not to scale
1000
500
0
METERS
THE ALLOTMENT
CLAPHAM BENTS
SULBER

The summit is flat but very rocky. There is a triangulation pillar and the 4-way shelter which gives some respite from the wind. On the top of it is a plaque depicting the views in all directions. In misty conditions or if disorientated, a compass bearing from the wind break of 80°m should take you back to the two cairns. Retrace your steps to the cairn marking the path to Horton which leads off right then take a compass bearing of 100°m to go downhill. The path has been repaired in parts over recent years and can be muddy in places.

Take the grass path with Pen-y-ghent in front and Horton down in the valley. Go over a stile. A sign pointing to Horton is just past it, followed by a large outcrop of limestone. This path runs between the limestone and undulating small hills, continue in a straight line towards Horton and Pen-y-ghent. Another signpost points back to Ingleborough and Horton 1½ miles (experience says it could be further), also to Sellside and Clapham.

Go over another stile and onto a stony path, through an opening in the stone wall, leading to a large expanse of limestone rocks. The path turns to the right, pick out your path here carefully. The large expanse of limestone rock diminishes and there are now fields usually containing animals.

Cross the fields following the narrow, undulating, worn trail with stiles over the stone walls. As you approach the railway line you see a sign for Horton in Ribblesdale at the small station. Cross the line with care and continue down the path and along the road ahead towards the car park in the village.

There is a small bridge over the river on your right. Go over this and you pass through the car park in Horton in Ribblesdale. The well known Pen-y-ghent café is nearby (this shop provides refreshments, outdoor equipment and tourist information). Turn right out of the car park and walk 45 metres to the café, then continue towards the church which you will see at the south end of the village. You will pass Holme Farm campsite on your right, cross the road.

Just past the campsite, turn left through a gate into a small field. The church is a short distance away. Proceed through the next gate in front of you and then turn left. You will see a wooden bridge over the stream about 35 metres further on. Cross over it then turn left onto a metalled road along by the local school.

Continue on the metalled road until you come to a farm where there is a signpost pointing to Pen-y-ghent summit. Turn left here, go over a stile and up by a stone wall. The grass path now starts to go steeply uphill, there are many ruts in the path.

Arriving at some stone steps in the wall ahead of you, Pen-y-ghent appears directly in front now. Over another wall and there is a large stone outcrop with some steps carved in it, go up these and continue generally along the side of the stone wall.

Looking back you can see Ingleborough in the distance with Horton in the valley and the quarry behind. At the base of Pen-y-ghent there are some steps as you continue to ascend steeply. Over two more stiles and you now have a view of the south side of Pen-y-ghent.

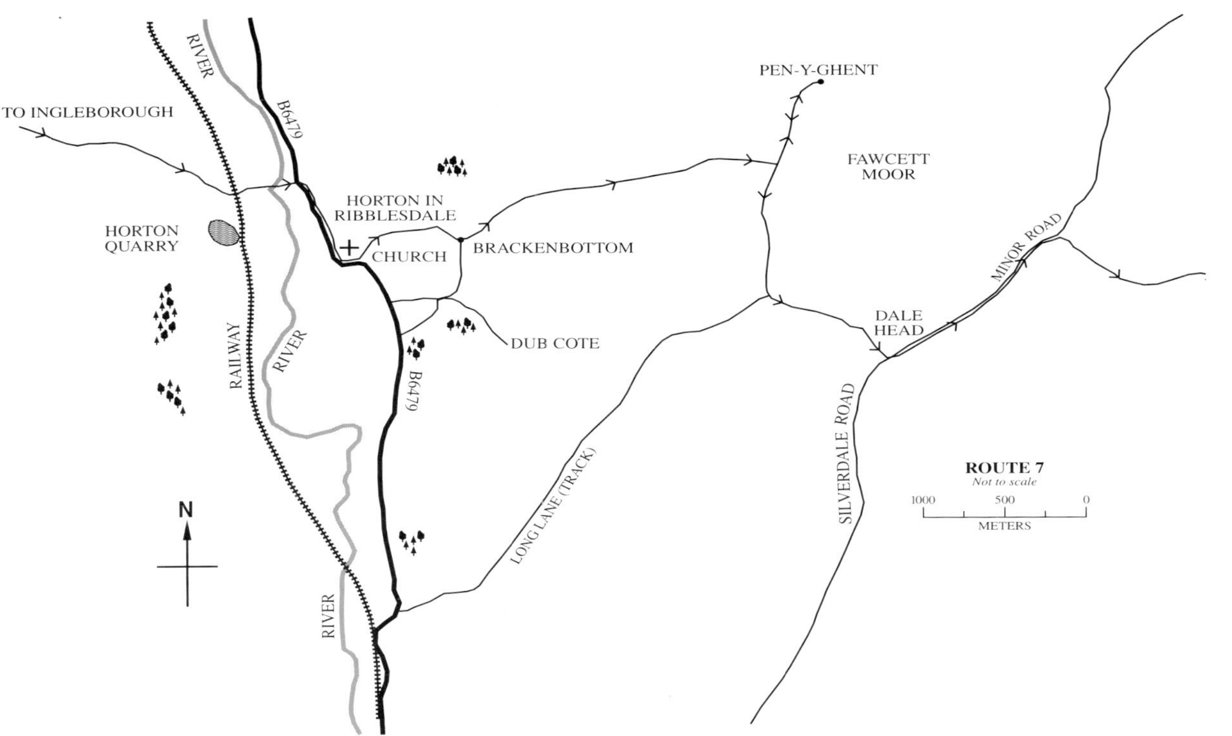
TO INGLEBOROUGH
RIVER
B6479
HORTON IN RIBBLESDALE
CHURCH
BRACKENBOTTOM
PEN-Y-GHENT
FAWCETT MOOR
HORTON QUARRY
RAILWAY
RIVER
DUB COTE
B6479
DALE HEAD
MINOR ROAD
SILVERDALE ROAD
LONG LANE (TRACK)
ROUTE 7
Not to scale
1000
500
0
METERS
N
RIVER

The shale and stone path to the summit is steep and care should be taken (plate 6). As you approach there are some steep steps up the large rock outcrop then the path begins to flatten out before coming to a walkway. The 'trig' point is in front of you on the summit. Enjoy the view in all directions.

On leaving Pen-y-ghent summit retrace your steps downhill. When you reach the steps over the stone wall do not take the path back to Horton but continue straight downhill on the Pennine Way. At Church Mill Hole the path bears left to Dale Head and a cattle grid on the road. Turn left and follow the Pennine Way along the road for 1400 metres to another cattle grid near a bend in the road. At this bend turn right, following a sign to Fountains Fell, still on the Pennine Way, to walk clockwise around the summit. Your path is obvious in parts but some parts are not distinguishable. The path leads along the side of a wall before branching off around the left side of the fell towards Arncliffe.

After you walk around the northerly side, you may see Fountains Fell Tarn off to your right as you begin to descend. Continue on the Pennine Way which now runs south east. The steep slopes of Fountains Fell are to your right and there are the remains of a stone wall as you proceed down to Tennets Gill. There are occasional piles of stones to mark the path, also a yellow arrow.

Just before Tennets Gill there is a stone wall with a stile and a 5 bar gate, go over this and pass the farm on the wide track towards the road.

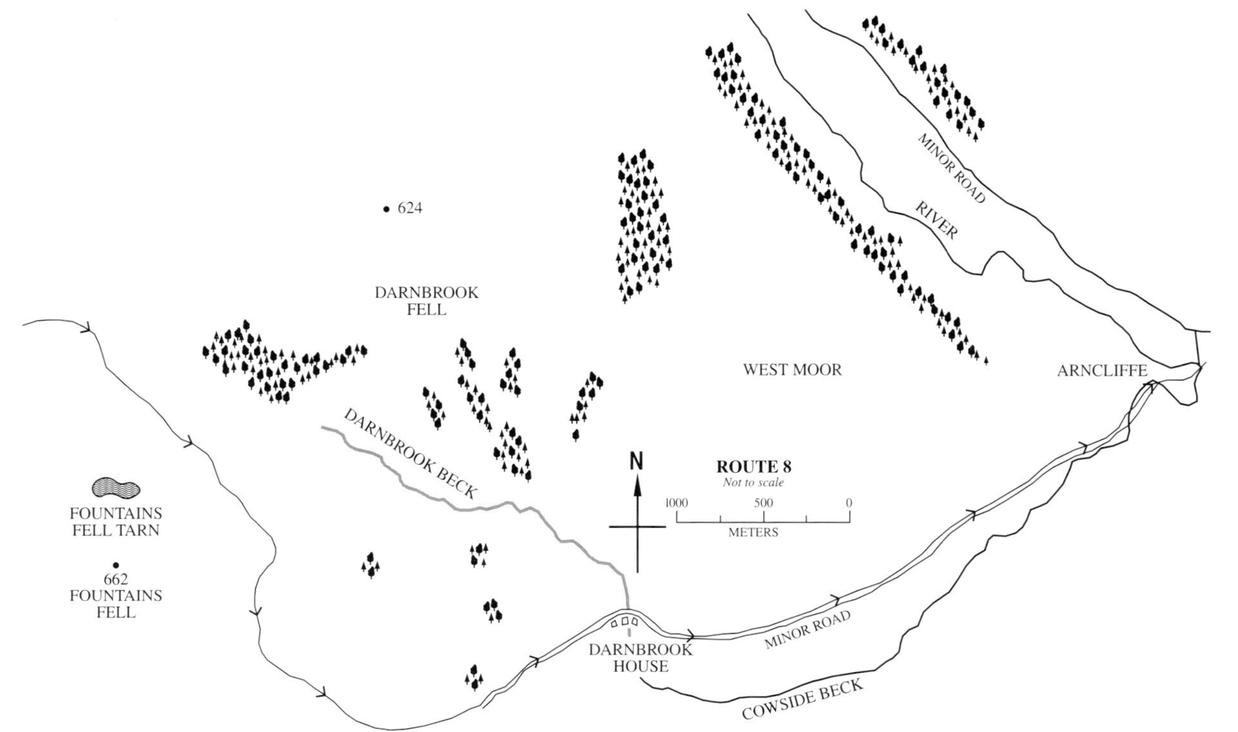
MINOR ROAD
RIVER
624
DARNBROOK FELL
WEST MOOR
ARNCLIFFE
DARNBROOK BECK
ROUTE 8
Not to scale
1000
500
0
METERS
N
FOUNTAINS FELL TARN
662
FOUNTAINS FELL
DARNBROOK HOUSE
MINOR ROAD
COWSIDE BECK

There is a cattle grid just before the road. Turn left walking for 5000 metres following the undulating road to Darnbrook House, then to Arncliffe. At the junction in Arncliffe turn left at the sign pointing to Kettlewell, just after you pass the church and school. Go over the bridge, there is a public footpath sign pointing to Kettlewell which goes over the steps in the stone wall and through a small gate. Follow the path to the next road, cross it, still following the signs to Kettlewell.

You begin to ascend 2 fields. Look for an opening in the wall ahead when diagonally crossing the next field. The stone and shale path has steep stone steps in it. You climb a waterfall following the well marked path. There are rocky outcrops of limestone in the next field as you ascend. Looking back there are good views to Arncliffe.

Cross some wooden steps over a stone wall where the path is not so visible, so look carefully for it. Use map and compass if necessary. A sign shows the footpath in both directions. Cross the gap in a stone wall and look for a sign showing the route. Continue ascending to the top of the hill on a grass path now. The ground can be wet here with springs.

Climb over a stile which takes you to some grass on level ground. Walk diagonally across the field to another stile over the wall. You may see Kettlewell in the valley. The grass path descends to another set of steps over a wall. You come to a farm track crossing your path. A sign points to Kettlewell.

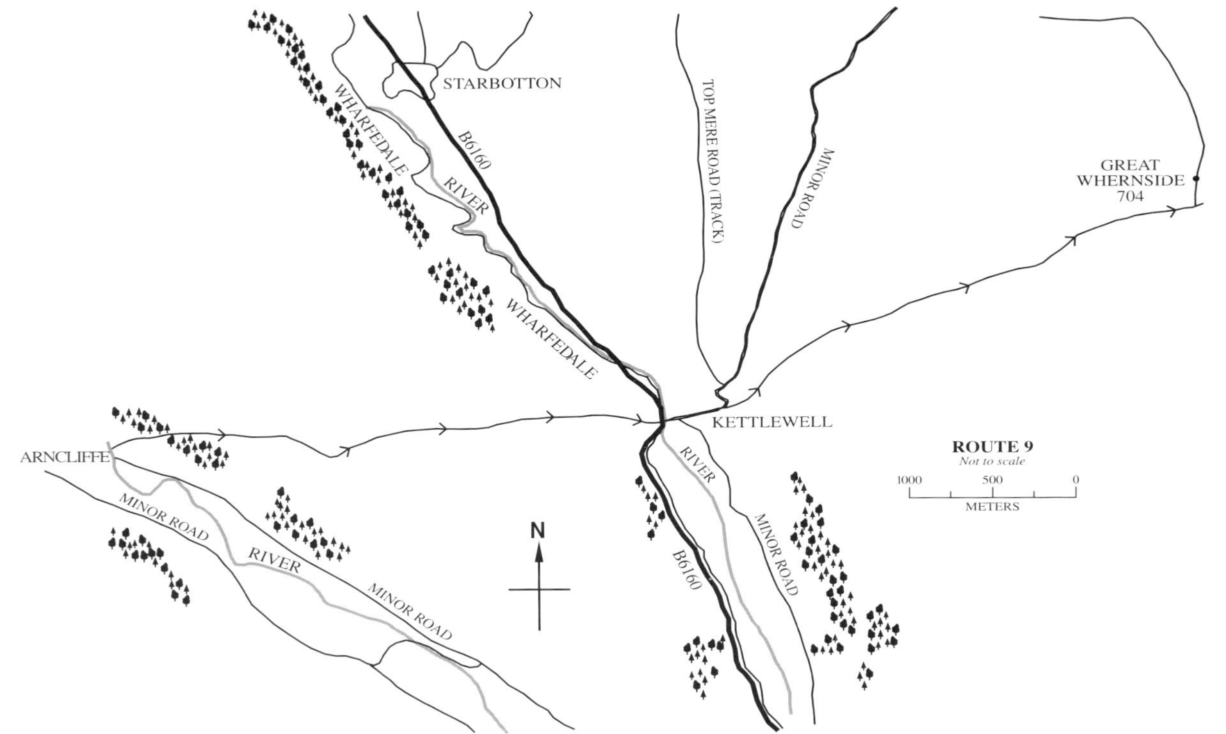
STARBOTTON
WHARFEDALE
B6160
RIVER
WHARFEDALE
TOP MERE ROAD (TRACK)
MINOR ROAD
GREAT
WHERNSIDE
704
KETTLEWELL
ROUTE 9
Not to scale
1000
500
0
METERS
ARNCLIFFE
MINOR ROAD
RIVER
MINOR ROAD
N
RIVER
B6160
MINOR ROAD

Your last section to Kettlewell is immediately below on a short steep descent. Take extra care going down a shale, then grass path. Cross the wooden steps over a wall and continue to another wall, then bear right along this wall, then through the gate into Kettlewell.

Cross the bridge and walk into the village, then to the campsite at the far side. The path ascends the grass fields on a public footpath/farm track (plate 13) to Hag Dyke 2100 metres above. This is a stiff climb. Once there, walk between the buildings, then follow the defined path to the 'trig' point, number 2976 on Great Whernside.

At the summit bear left on 9°m to take you between the grass and large stones to Blackfell Top, where there is a wind shelter.

Continue on the path to Black Dike End where there are 2 paths, one going left the other straight across. Turn left here bearing 269°m from this junction. This will take you downhill over 3 stiles to the road which you should see at the bottom. Cross the road following a sign to Buckden Pike on bearing 304°m. You walk along the side of a wall, then bear right along the side of another wall, still gradually ascending. The ground can be wet in parts.

You pass a memorial on the hillside in memory of an airman and a plane crash (plate 12). Follow the wall along to the summit of Buckden Pike. A white 'trig' point is numbered 5520 (plate 11).

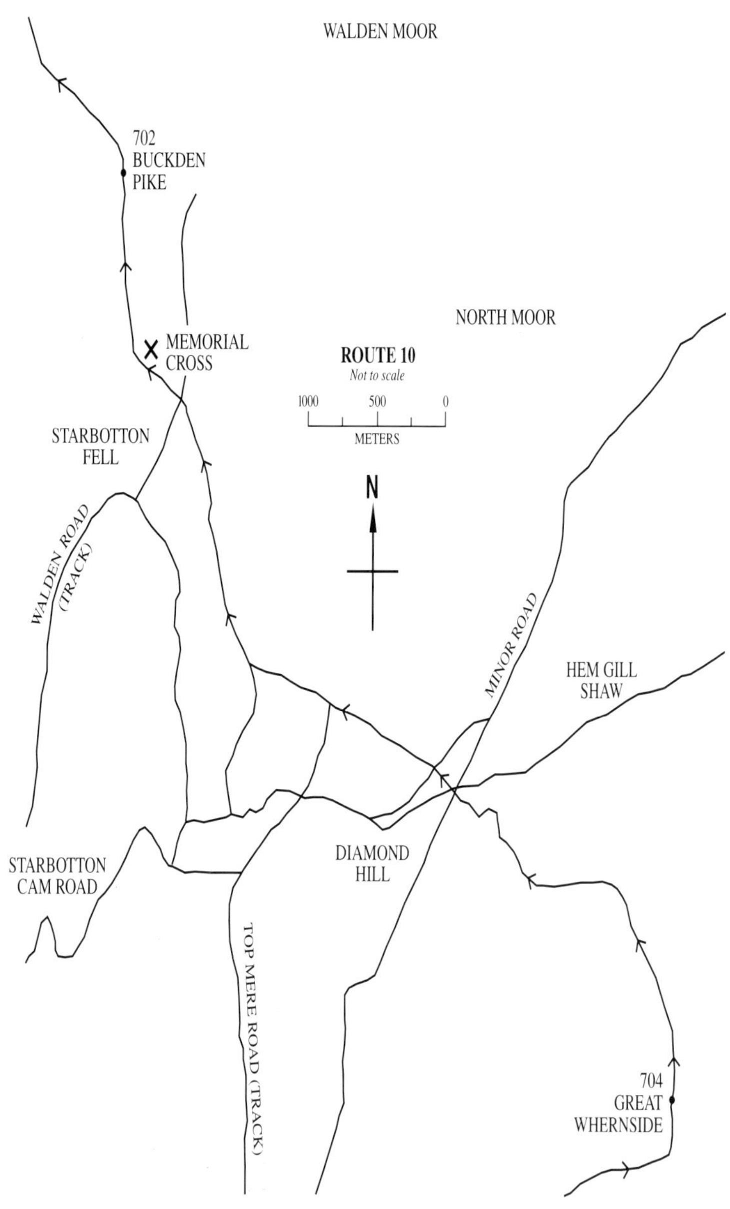
WALDEN MOOR
702
BUCKDEN
PIKE
MEMORIAL
CROSS
NORTH MOOR
ROUTE 10
Not to scale
1000
500
0
METERS
N
STARBOTTON
FELL
WALDEN ROAD
(TRACK)
MINOR ROAD
HEM GILL
SHAW
DIAMOND
HILL
STARBOTTON
CAM ROAD
TOP MERE ROAD (TRACK)
704
GREAT
WHERNSIDE

Leaving the 'trig' point on bearing 5°m cross the stile, then bear 313°m leading north west and descending to a road 2500 metres away. The path descends by a wall. Walk towards the thin line of woodland in the direction of Bainbridge.

When you arrive at the road cross it, then ascend steeply to the top of the wood, keeping to the left side of it. There is no visible path but keep in the general direction 327°m. You come to a distinctive track known as Gilbert Lane. Walk along, then over a stile onto Stake Moss which has a lot of shake holes or large stones.

Your route comes to a farm gate with a stile on the left and a sign stating footpath. Take this left path bearing 348°m. The grass track which is just visible descends, then climb a stile over a stone wall leading to Stalling Busk on a good grass track.

Walk through a gate between a stone wall, going downhill. The track winds down the side of a stream on your right side. You come to a ruined sheep pen and beside it a wall with a stone step which you go over. Go over another step and there is a broken down stone wall ahead as you descend. It is difficult to see the path here but there is an opening with a step over the wall. On the lower side of the wall you can pick up a definite path going downhill.

You cross a wide stream known as Shaw Gate Gill where you should see the path on the other side of it. As you ascend the gentle slope you will see a stile over the stone wall in front of you. At this point

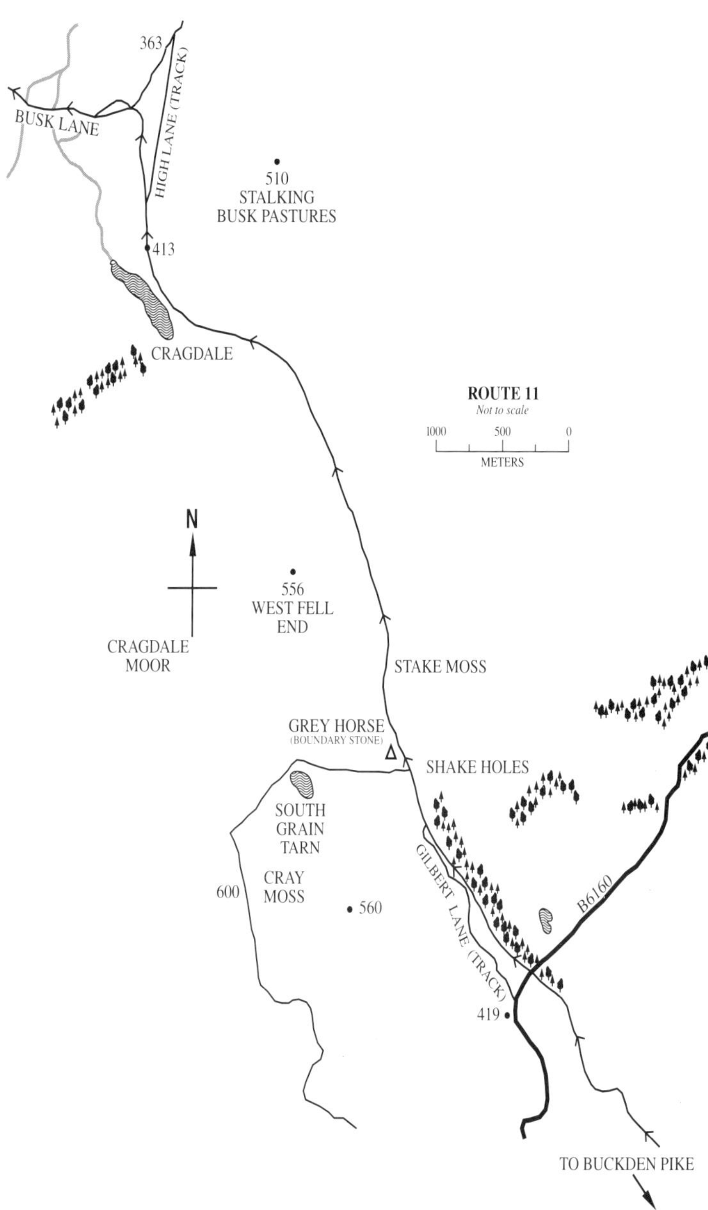
363
HIGH LANE (TRACK)
BUSK LANE
510
STALKING
BUSK PASTURES
413
CRAGDALE
ROUTE 11
Not to scale
1000
500
0
METERS
N
556
WEST FELL
END
CRAGDALE
MOOR
STAKE MOSS
GREY HORSE
(BOUNDARY STONE)
SHAKE HOLES
SOUTH
GRAIN
TARN
CRAY
MOSS
600
560
GILBERT LANE (TRACK)
B6160
419
TO BUCKDEN PIKE

you are walking along the edge of a grass hillside with a steep drop off to your left, so take care. A farm gate is at the top of the hillside. Walk through and turn left onto a rough stone and shale track known as Bob Lane Track.

You come to the village of Stalling Busk. Follow the road left at the village round to the church. Opposite the church is Busk Lane Track. Walk down this wide rutted track of stone and shale for a short distance. The path widens with grass at each side. You come to a sign saying public footpath with an opening between a stone wall on your right. Walk through, then bear left following a path downhill towards Marcett Village. You may see the village on the opposite hill in front and the path leading to it.

There is a barn in the lower part of the valley and another footpath joins you from the right. You should now see a definite grass path ahead. Follow this to a stone wall. There is a wooden gate with a yellow arrow on it, walk through and continue over 2 fields and a bridge. Walk on a stone and shale path, with a stream on your right, towards Marcett.

Do not go into the village but cross Marcett bridge on your right. There is a public footpath on your left, do not take this but walk along the road a short distance to a farm track on your left with a signpost showing Hawes and Buttersett. Walk along this lane to the end of the track then the public footpath branches off to Hawes. There is a farm gate with an arrow pointing towards Hawes. The general direction is 309°m.

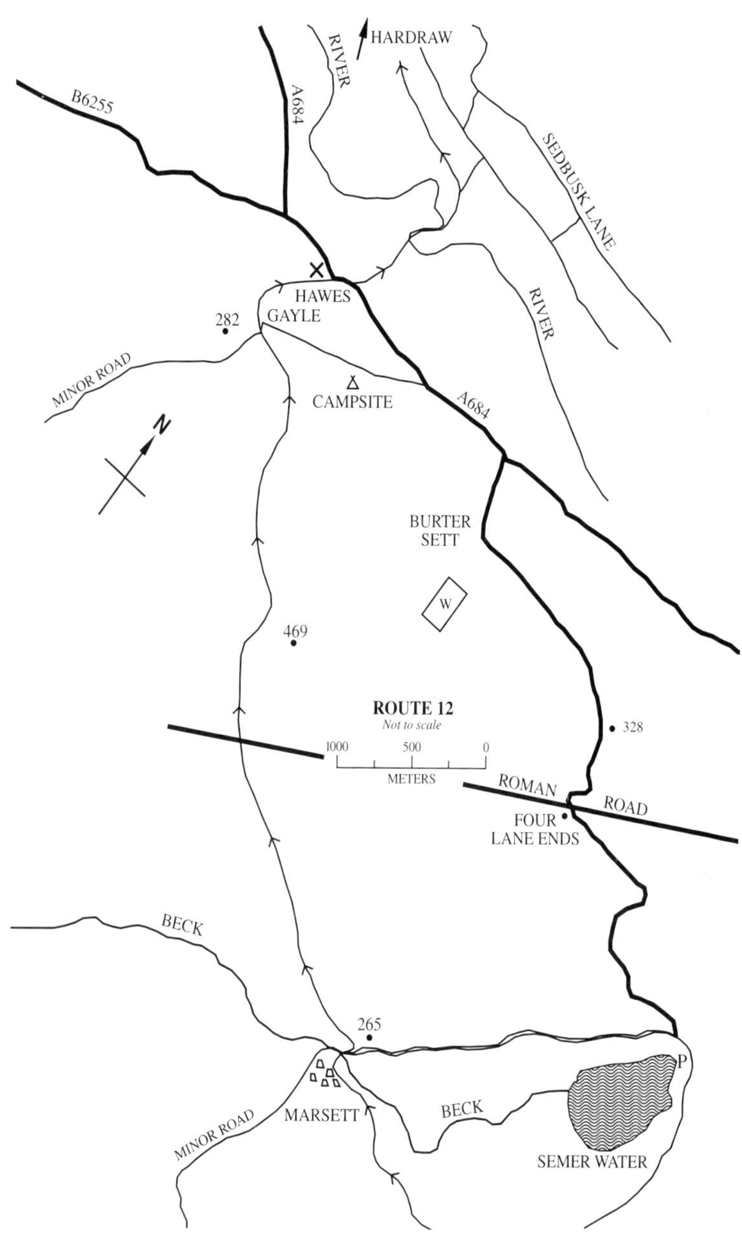
HARDRAW
RIVER
A684
B6255
SEDBUSK LANE
HAWES
GAYLE
282
RIVER
MINOR ROAD
CAMPSITE
A684
N
BURTER
SETT
W
469
ROUTE 12
Not to scale
1000
500
0
METERS
328
ROMAN
ROAD
FOUR
LANE ENDS
BECK
265
P
MARSETT
BECK
MINOR ROAD
SEMER WATER

You ascend over several fields and through 3 openings in the stone walls. The path is clear in some areas but disappears in others. Walk uphill to a broken stone wall, continue to another stone wall, then bear off 311°m to take you around the left side of a hill named Yorburgh, towards Hawes.

Your path descends now and you will probably see Hawes in the distance ahead. Your path becomes more visible as you descend the hill. Keep walking in the general direction of 311°m to take you to the bridge in Gayle, then turn right to Hawes Centre. Walk around the side of the church in Hawes, then turn right. Cross the one-way system and follow the signs to Hardraw.

Walk along this road by the side of the museum and you will pick up the Pennine Way path, follow this over the stile into a field. Go through the gate at the far end, back onto the road, then walk cautiously around the bend and over the bridge. Do not turn off onto the first public footpath marked Appersett or on the second marked Hardraw but continue to the far side of the river, then turn left onto the Pennine Way back to Hardraw. There are 5 steps up and a sign, at this turn off in the road.

Continue on this path through the field on some stone slabs and over some stiles until you arrive at Hardraw Village.

You have now completed The Yorkshire Dales Top Ten. ***Congratulations!***

ESCAPE ROUTES

During the ascent of any mountain care should be taken especially in bad visibility.

As stated earlier more accidents happen on the return journey than on the outward on. It may be difficult to pick out the path of descent in low cloud or in darkness. In situations like this follow the bearings and details below to ensure a safe descent from the summit.

Taking these bad visibility routes may not bring you to your desired destination, but will ensure you descend to a place of shelter from high ground in bad weather or other emergency.

Great Shunner Fell - G.R. 849973

The shortest and easiest route to a road is from the 'trig' point along the Pennine Way bearing 236°m initially for 460 metres, then a general bearing 191°m following the obvious path descending to Hardraw.

High Seat - G.R. 802012

The safest route to a road at low level is from the summit bearing 359°m. Follow the boundary fence for 1700 metres before bearing north north-easterly 29°m for 1750 metres to the road near Hollow Mill Cross.

Swarth Fell - G.R. 756966

At Swarth Fell summit bearing 331°m, follow a boundary wall for 600 metres then bear right 125°m descending 750 metres. Turn easterly 84°m for 1680 metres descending to the road at Cotegill Bridge.

Great Coum - G.R.701836

At the summit bear 116°m, descend for 1050 metres along a boundary wall to an old road/bridleway. Reaching this point turn left, following the obvious bridleway for 1700 metres, at a junction with Green Lane Track. Bear right on Nun House Outrake for 1650 metres to the road at Peacock Hill.

Crag Hill - G.R. 692833

The most direct path descends to a road at G.R. 668848 and is from the 'trig' point bearing 320°m north-westerly. Follow a boundary fence in that general direction for 3450 metres to reach the road.

Whernside - G.R. 738814

The shortest route from Whernside summit to the nearest road at G.R. 722818 is in a westerly direction bearing 281°m. Follow a path for 900 metres downhill, then turn northerly for 150 metres on bearing 19°m. Take a westerly bearing 284°m following a wall downhill to the road for 1150 metres.

Ingleborough - G.R. 741746

The shortest route to a road at lower level is to the Old Hill Inn at G.R. 743776. Turn from the summit on 72°m for 700 metres going quickly downhill. After going through the gate pick up a path going directly downhill bearing 352°m from the gate, off the peak towards Humphrey Bottom. Follow the path in the general direction back to the Old Hill Inn. (Extreme caution down the zig-zag path).

Pen-y-ghent - G.R. 839734

The shortest route from Pen-y-ghent summit to the nearest road at G.R. 843714 is S.S.W. from the summit bearing 221°m on the Pennine Way and turning in a south-easterly direction after 1620 metres on bearing 112°m for a further 1000 metres.

Great Whernside - G.R. 002739

The most straightforward although not the shortest route to a road is from the trig point towards Kettlewell on a general bearing of 252°m. Follow a distinct path down for 3800 metres to reach the village.

Buckden Pike - G.R. 961788

At the trig point bear 5°m for 100 metres then 311°m north-westerly following the general direction of the path descending for 3800 metres to a road at G.R. 945806.

It is important to re-state that all bearings given in these emergency descent routes are magnetic bearings. Magnetic north is estimated at 5° west of grid north in 1999 decreasing by about ½° in four years.

APPENDIX

USEFUL INFORMATION

Campsites on Route - in route order

Hardraw Campsite	G.R. 867912
Near Holme Heads Bridge on A684	G.R. 853913
Cobbles Hill off A684/B6259	G.R. 801930
Ewegales	G.R. 755868
Old Hill Inn at Chapel le Dale	G.R. 743776
Holme Farm Site, Horton in Ribblesdale	G.R. 809723
Kettlewell	G.R. 974725
Hawes	G.R. 880894

Walkers intending to walk the top ten circular over a number of days should note that there are large gaps between campsites. This may necessitate a wild camp at certain places. Try to use official campsites where possible.

Walking Times Between Prominent Landmarks

	Hours	Mins
Hardraw Campsite to Great Shunner Fell	2	15
Great Shunner Fell to High Seat	2	55
High Seat to Swarth Fell	4	15
Swarth Fell to Great Coum	3	45
Great Coum to Crag Hill	0	15
Crag Hill to Whernside	2	15
Whernside to Ingleborough	2	40
Ingleborough to Horton in Ribblesdale	2	15
Horton in Ribblesdale to Pen-y-ghent	1	10
Pen-y-ghent to Kettlewell	5	00
Kettlewell to Great Whernside	1	43
Great Whernside to Buckden Pike	2	45
Buckden Pike to Hardraw	7	00
	38 hours	

Note: Walking the complete route will take approximately 38 hours pure walking time. This will depend on fitness of the group and the conditions encountered. Walking the ten highest peaks in succession is a stiff task for anyone while carrying full equipment.

Distances Between Prominent Landmarks -
Calculated to include ascents and descents.

	Miles	Metres
Hardraw Campsite to Great Shunner Fell	4.84	7,860
Great Shunner Fell to High Seat	4.74	7,700
High Seat to Swarth Fell	6.39	10,380
Swarth Fell to Great Coum	14.40	23,400
Great Coum to Crag Hill	0.60	1,000
Crag Hill to Whernside	4.64	7,540
Whernside to Ingleborough	5.47	8,880
Ingleborough to Pen-y-ghent	7.66	12,450
Pen-y-ghent to Great Whernside	14.47	23,470
Great Whernside to Buckden Pike	4.60	7,480
Buckden Pike to Hardraw	11.85	19,250
	79.66	129,410

The Yorkshire Dales Top Ten involves walking nearly 80 miles in total. A good degree of fitness and navigational skills are required along with general experience of the outdoor environment.

Heights of Peaks

	Metres	Feet
Great Shunner Fell	716	2327
High Seat	709	2304
Swarth Fell	681	2213
Great Coum	687	2233
Crag Hill	682	2216
Whernside	736	2392
Ingleborough	723	2350
Pen-y-ghent	694	2255
Great Whernside	704	2288
Buckden Pike	702	2281

Nearest Telephones on Route

Hardraw Village

Aisgill Moor Cottages

Garsdale Head

Garsdale

Cowgill

Old Hill Inn, Chapel le Dale

Horton in Ribblesdale

Arncliffe

Kettlewell

Buckden

Stalling Busk

Marcett

Gayle

Hawes

Useful Addresses

Long Distance Walkers Association

Brian Smith
10 Temple Park Close, Leeds LS15 0JJ
Tel: 0113 264 2205

This association is set up to further the interests of those who enjoy long distance walking. Members receive a journal three times each year which includes information on all aspects of long distance walking.

Ramblers Association

1-5 Wandsworth Road, London SW8 2XX
Advice and information on all walking matters.
Local groups with regular meetings.

The Yorkshire Dales National Park and Tourist Information Centres

Aysgarth Falls	01969 663424
Clapham	015242 51419
Grassington	01756 752774
Hawes	01969 667450
Malham	01729 830363
Sedbergh	015396 20125
Pen-y-ghent Café, Horton in Ribblesdale	01729 860333
Ingleton	015242 41049
Settle	01729 825192

Glossary of Words

Bearing - *A degree or number of degrees set on a compass then follow the direction of travel arrow to walk on that bearing to reach your intended destination.*

Cairn - *An ancient stone mound erected as a marker. Often modern day piles of stones are referred to as cairns. This is not the case but many people use this expression when referring to piles of stones that denote a path or route.*

Col - *A pass or saddle between two hills. It provides access between one valley and another.*

Crag - *A steep rugged rock or peak.*

Escape Route - *Used for any emergency situation or in times of bad visibility. The main aim is to get you down to lower ground by the safest and quickest way.*

Grid Reference - *Derived from the national grid reference system. This is used to pinpoint a place on a map by the use of letters and numbers.*

Kissing Gate - *Swing gate that usually lets one person through it at a time by moving the gate backwards and forwards.*

Magnetic Bearing - *This is a grid bearing taken from a map and the relevant magnetic variation added to it to obtain the magnetic bearing. See the relevant maps for details of current magnetic variation.*

Metalled Road - *Generally known as a stone chipping road. This term evolved and became regarded as the roads metal or the roads surface.*

Outcrop - *Part of a rock formation that sticks out from the main body of rock.*

Plateau - *A wide and mainly flat area of elevated land.*

Route Card - *A plan of action prepared before you leave. A copy to be left with someone so that if you fail to return by a planned time then help can be summoned.*

Summit - *The highest point of a mountain or hill.*

Tarn - *A small mountain lake. Water from the mountains runs down and is caught in a land lock, so creating a tarn.*

Trig Point - *True name is Triangulation Pillar. These mark the summit of many mountains but not all the top ten have one. It is a small stone pillar with a number on it. The height of the mountain is taken from this point.*